HOW TO SAVE £10,000 ON A LOW INCOME

A NO-NONSENSE GUIDE TO MONEY MANAGEMENT

Annette Galloway

"Your wealth can only grow according to the level of your financial literacy."

Anne Wilson

For the 12.7 million households in debt and the 1 in 4 adults with no savings

ISBN - 978-1-80049-097-0

Printed in the United Kingdom

Independently Published

Disclaimer: The information in this book is for educational purposes and is to be used as a guide. For specific investment advice or recommendations please speak to a qualified financial adviser.

TABLE OF CONTENTS

ACKNOWLEDGEMENTS

I am thankful to my mother, who taught me a powerful life lesson in money management when she got into debt when I was a child. She then paid it back and never got into debt again. I learned to manage money well because of this.

I am thankful for all the individuals in my savings group who are saving money consistently based on our savings challenges. I am also grateful for all of those individuals who have joined the Rapid Wealth Building Platform. They have trusted me to help them, on a daily basis, to be more financially secure. They have believed that financial security is possible, and they are working hard to achieve this. I am also grateful for all the testimonials I have received from people who have cleared debt or who are currently paying off debt, saving money consistently and have invested, or are on their way to becoming investors.

I am grateful to God, who has permitted me to live a life that is full of meaning and purpose. I experience a new lease of life when I speak about financial literacy. I can't imagine wanting to do anything else. **Mark Twain summed this up well when he said: "The two most important days in your life are the day you are born, and the day you find out why."** The day I discovered my purpose back in the autumn of 2018, on the back of a prayer, is the day I truly began to live a life of meaning and purpose. I will be forever grateful for that day. I hope you discover that day too.

I am thankful for Blessing Theophilus Israel, who has supported me relentlessly as a mentor, friend, and coach. I am also grateful for Carol Williams, who helps me bring financial literacy to the people on our wealth building platform daily. I am also grateful to all the people who have helped me along the journey. Men such as Bishop Creswell Green from Latter-Rain Church in Peckham, who allowed me to use his church at no cost when I first began delivering financial literacy workshops. I am also grateful for John Ozibona, who has acted as a sounding board for this book. I am grateful to Edem Amewowor, the Financial Advisor I work with, who is just as passionate as I am about bringing financial literacy to the nation. He is a gifted financial adviser and an excellent teacher. I am also grateful to Tunji Olujimi, who runs a company called Accelerated Authors Academy. They designed the book cover and published this book. They have done an amazing job.

ABOUT ME

Hello, aspiring wealth builder. My name is Annette Galloway. I have a BA degree in Sociology and History. I am a Financial Educator. I am the mother of a young son. In my spare time, I enjoy exercising, travelling, and exploring new places. I am committed to my own personal growth and development and enjoy taking on new challenges. I believe there is the potential to learn something new every day.

I am passionate about financial literacy. I run a company called Saver to Investor. The motto is: Make Money, Save Money, Invest Money. The goal is to encourage people to manage money better so they can begin saving and then go on to invest confidently.

Main Goal

The ultimate goal of Saver to Investor is to encourage 100,000 people to increase their financial literacy so that they begin to clear debt, save money on a regular basis, build their net worth and empower themselves to invest their money confidently.

I hope you choose to be one of these 100,000 wealth builders. The goal of this book is to encourage and empower you through my personal story and the money principles in this book, to get a hold of your finances. Everyone deserves financial security. No one should have to suffer the harsh consequences of debt or poor money management.

Financial security comes from good money management; however, investing is the source of true financial freedom. You can begin to build wealth through saving and investing regularly on a low income. I want to inspire you to do the same. If I achieved this, so can you!

Some goals I expect this book will help you to achieve are:

1. Increase your financial literacy
2. Save money on a regular basis
3. Build up a Freedom Fund to £1000 as quickly as possible
4. Pay off consumer debt as quickly as possible
5. Get you to understand **WHY** you want financial freedom
6. Set financial goals that you will achieve
7. Develop a better relationship with money
8. Improve your credit score
9. Calculate your net worth

10. Save money and then invest. Investment is where financial freedom resides!

I have given you several **Wealth Building Exercises** in this book that I also give out to the wealth builders on the Rapid Wealth Building Forum that I run. The wealth builders are individuals who desire to build wealth. They are aiming to leave a financial legacy to their family and friends. I run this group alongside my colleague Carol Williams. I hope these exercises help you to make progress on the financial adventure you are currently undertaking. I trust that they will help you to begin saving thousands of pounds over the next few years just like I have done.

My Story

My mum experienced debt when I was nine years old. After seeing the impact of debt in her life, I vowed to never be in debt, no matter my income level. I managed to save thousands of pounds a year as a single parent, regardless of the income coming in. At times, my income ranged from £18,000 to £25,000; sometimes, it was bit less. I had quite a lot of overheads and childcare fees and still managed to save a few thousand a year for my son and me. I began D.I.Y investing in funds nearly two years ago, having taught myself from reading books. I mainly invest in exchange traded funds. To be on the safe side, I also take advice from a qualified financial adviser. I am pleased to say that my investments have far surpassed the returns on a typical savings account, which are currently on average 0.65% at today's rates. Most banks today won't give you a 1% return on your hard-earned cash for most savings accounts! As such, investing is a no-brainer.

My mum's debt accrued from two televisions and two single mattresses, which she purchased for a total cost of around £600 in the mid 1990's. She took out credit to pay for these items. She couldn't afford to consistently make payments beyond the minimum amount to clear the credit, so she eventually got into debt. This is quite a common problem. She began struggling financially, and the debt wasn't reducing in size due to the interest being charged. The rate of interest was about 20% APR. The debt was growing in size because interest was being added to the debt, and then more interest was being applied on top. This was occurring on a monthly basis, so her small debt was snowballing out of control.

My mum experienced the negative impact of a powerful concept called **compound interest.** This means that the debt company was making her **pay interest on interest**, so the debt was quickly spiralling out of control. The goal of good money management is to get compound interest working in your finances positively. This would mean that your savings or investments are growing over time, through interest being added to interest. Over time, compound interest helps your savings grow significantly.

I have the concept of compound interest working in my savings and investments. It is also working in my son's savings and investments. This is the outcome I want you to achieve.

Debt spiralling out of control is quite a common issue. My mum decided to ask the debt company to freeze the interest payments on the debt so she could pay the amount completely. Fortunately, they agreed to this request. When she finally cleared the total balance of the debt, she vowed that she would never get into debt again, and she never did. Having experienced the emotional impact of my mum's debt as a young child, and seeing the impact of that debt on my mum and siblings, it had the positive effect of causing me to want to handle money very well. As a result, I never have experienced debt. I wish to teach as many people as possible good money management skills so they can achieve similar results.

I worked as a teaching assistant and lived with my mum before my son was born when I was 25. Before my son was born, I was cash-rich because I lived at home and didn't have to pay much towards household expenses. Saving money was effortless. I used the money principles discussed in this book to save several thousand pounds. When I had my own household to run at 25, while raising my young son, I had a lot of overheads to pay. I returned to work when my son was three and a half years old. Nurseries typically charged between £1,000 and £1,200 a month for a child to attend full time. That is quite a lot of money, especially when your household income isn't that high or if you are raising a child as a single parent. The government assisted and paid quite a large part of the nursery fees, but the remaining fees were quite expensive in relation to my salary of £18,000 per year as an Administrator.

I have to humble myself to admit this, but I was entitled to top-up payments for my daily living from the government, alongside help with childcare costs, despite working full time. Despite my low income, I still saved. In my case, my savings journey was slow and steady, rather than fast. **Slow and steady can win the race!** I want to assure you that you can still have a low income and begin achieving financial security. The journey will just take longer unless you find a way to increase your revenue. At times you will have to find a way to bring in more money to get quicker results with regards to building up your savings. This could be through a pay rise or getting a side hustle.

It is ok to get slow results, especially when you know that you will eventually begin investing. Investing is fantastic because it has the capacity to grow your finances quite quickly in comparison to just saving money. While earning £18,000 a year, each month I saved what I could afford. This was typically £80 a month for my son and £200 a month for myself. When I began earning £25,000,

I could save more. I saved on average £120 for my son and £350 for myself. I felt like the working poor because despite earning £25,000 a year, I was entitled to assistance for childcare and a small payment towards daily living costs. And you guessed it, I still saved and then began investing. My capacity to save consistently was based on the budgeting model that I will introduce you to soon, as well as following three money principles, which will help you do the same. The only problem was that I didn't know how to invest and didn't feel comfortable approaching a financial adviser based on a negative experience I had with a financial adviser at the age of 23. I delayed investing for nearly ten years because of this. This is why I am so passionate about teaching people about money management and investing. I want people to feel confident to have a financial conversation with a financial adviser and to be in the position to actually invest.

Each person has their own unique individual circumstances. **I believe most people can save £10,000. All you need is a mindset for wealth creation, to live from a budget, begin implementing money principles, begin clearing your debt, and then track your net worth at least monthly.**

My hope for you reading this book is that you eventually secure your financial freedom through investing. I hope you regard yourself as one of the 100,000 wealth builders

I am aiming to help and join us on this powerful wealth-building journey! You do not have to live a lifetime of financial chaos. You can be financially secure, but it requires sacrifice, time, commitment, money, and consistency.

I want as many people as possible to achieve financial freedom. Financial freedom means you have enough passive income coming in to cover your living expenses. Passive income means that you do not have to be physically present at a job to earn money. Financial freedom means that you have the choice as to whether or not you want to continue working. Investing is a way you can begin to achieve financial freedom. Saving is not sufficient on its own because the interest you receive when saving your hard-earned money is very low (typically less than 1%). The rates for potential growth are a lot higher when investing. Risk is involved, but this risk can be managed with good financial advice and financial literacy.

I have shared my personal story with you because I want you to get results. It has taken a lot of humility to share my story. I have done so because if I can save and invest more than 10% of my salary when I was earning a low income, so can you. There are really no excuses. You can save money on a low income and even as a single parent, low-income household. I have absolute faith that you can get the same results and more. **I hope to reach at least**

100,000 low-income individuals or households with this book to empower these people to begin building financial security on a low income through saving money and good money management and through tracking their net worth. Let's do this! As you read this book, I trust you will be empowered to save £10,000 and be motivated to begin eventually investing so that you can build your net worth. I have a free savings Telegram group you can join to encourage you to save consistently. Please get in touch for more details.

NOTES PAGE

CHAPTER 1

MINDSET

Your Money Story

There is a common saying that states that where your focus goes, your energy flows. This is true regarding money. We all have a money story we tell ourselves daily. It affects how we see money. Unfortunately, many people see it from a standpoint of scarcity and lack. The money story they tell themselves is negative and is often based on some of the toxic things they have been told about money by their parents or other adults in their community as children. As a child, I was told by adults that money doesn't grow on trees, that they couldn't afford to buy a certain item, or that rich people were evil or greedy. Despite the things I used to hear, deep down, I believed that one day I would be very comfortable financially and most likely would eventually be rich! I began to tell myself a positive money story. **I told myself that no matter what happened to my income, I would never be broke or poor or in debt.** I told myself that I would always be content with the money I had and would always live within my means. **I also told myself I would have thousands of pounds in savings.** Because of my positive money story, based on the powerful affirmations I told myself, I have never struggled with money. **You get what you focus on.** My positive money story is backed up by strong money affirmations, alongside me knowing **WHY** I want financial security. We will look at your **WHY** later on in the book. **My WHY and my money goals have been placed on my vision board.** I look at and meditate on my financial vision board daily.

In order to get ahead financially, we need to tell ourselves a positive money story. We need to acknowledge some of the negative stories we tell ourselves about money and replace them with something positive.

Wealth Building Exercise: Take a moment to ask yourself what money story you have been telling yourself. What views do you hold? Write them all down, and if they are negative, replace them with something more positive and empowering. Once you have some positive empowering statements regarding money, you can turn them into money affirmations.

For example: "I believe that I will always be broke" could be replaced with "If I manage money well, I will be financially stable."

The first statement regarding always being broke doesn't empower you to take action. The second statement regarding managing money better empowers you to take action by acknowledging that if you manage money well, you will become financially stable.

Putting yourself first

Putting yourself first is a very important habit. At times, in order to avoid being selfish, we are told to put others first. This is quite a noble idea but in practice it can be quite dangerous, especially with regards to your finances. To truly prosper, you need to look after yourself first, and then you can be of use to everyone else. I grew up in inner-city London amongst lots of African and Caribbean people. I had African friends whose parents regularly sent money back home. This is quite common. My mother is white English, so I was always grateful knowing that I wouldn't have to send money back home as I knew that this held back many people's finances. If this is an issue for you, there is a solution to it, although it will take logic and willpower to implement.

As a teenager, I had a friend, who when she got her first job, was expected to dutifully send money back home to Africa for various relatives' needs, such as food, clothing, funerals, weddings, etc. – sometimes at short notice. The problem was that there was always a relative in need of financial assistance. I have another adult friend, let's call her Nicole, who recently asked me for my view regarding sending money back home to Africa. Nicole told me her savings had been badly depleted because a relative was ill and needed to travel overseas for surgery. She had already donated a lot of money, and she said this had nearly eaten into all of her savings. I explained to her that her family did not know how much money she had, and even if they did, she wasn't obliged to send all her savings back home, even if it was for a family emergency. I told Nicole to set aside a particular amount of money that she wanted to donate for a specific period of time for family requests for financial assistance. I advised her that once she had given this money away, to not give away any more. I suggested that she act as if there was no more money to give. I told her that by putting others first, she was compromising her own financial security, which would mean she wouldn't make any financial progress.

This reasoning made sense to Nicole. She could see that in trying to put others first, she had not put herself first financially and kept on ending up with little or no savings. She realised that this was becoming a vicious cycle that only she could break. She said this situation had happened more than once. I told her it could possibly happen again if she didn't take suitable action. **She decided to let logic dominate her emotions, and she is now financially stable.** Nicole put in place a small pot of money that she was willing to give to her family each month. She decided on the amount she felt comfortable with. When that money was used up, she didn't pay out anything more. She understood that giving more money compromised her financial progress. **She still had peace of mind knowing that she gave what she could afford, rather than giving for the sake of giving, at her own expense. She is now saving consistently and is also investing her way to financial freedom.** The moral of the story here is that in order to succeed, you need to win first. You need to put yourself ahead of others so that you can help them where you can while still achieving your own financial goals.

With a lift of his chin and a bit of a grin, Without any doubting or 'quit-it'.

He started to sing as he tackled the thing That couldn't be done. And he did it.

Edgar A. Guest

Limiting beliefs

The verse above is an extract from a poem by Edgar Guest. **It neatly summarises how people say something can't be done until someone achieves it.** People will make excuses for anything. For being in debt, not have savings, over-spending, not investing, etc. **At a particular time in your life, you have to make up your mind to set a goal and be committed to achieving it.** It would be a great powerful movement if 100,000 got behind this book and began putting together a plan to save £10,000 like I have done. It may take you one year, two years, three years, seven years, or maybe even ten years. Take as long as you need, but get it done! **Just don't forget to invest a portion of it when you have saved it and seek help when investing if necessary.**

Running a mile in under four minutes

Before 1954 men and women the world over believed that you could not run a mile in under four minutes simply because it hadn't been done before. On 6 May 1954, Roger Bannister broke the four-minute barrier, running the distance in three minutes and 59.4 seconds.

Barely a year after Bannister's accomplishment, someone else ran a mile in under four minutes. Now, it's almost routine, with college students running a mile in under four minutes.

What does this tell us?

You can achieve what you have set your mind to achieve. I had a low income with a young son to look after. I set a goal to save over £10,000 for my son and myself, and I easily achieved it. I surpassed this goal. **Set a goal and expect to achieve it. The only thing that can stop you**

is you. You could choose to save a lower amount than £10,000. Any amount of savings are better than no savings. I was once told by a colleague that she couldn't possibly save any of her salary because she didn't earn enough. She earned over £25,000, and she and her young child lived with her partner, who also worked full-time. However, she spent lots of money on eating out daily for lunch, she smoked, and would buy expensive perfume that she left on her desk. I assured her she could save. I was going to tell her to consider how much she spent on x, y, and z, but I could tell that she didn't want to change. She wasn't emotionally prepared for change, and I had the wisdom to keep quiet. When you are ready to make a goal and commit to your goal, there is no reason why you can't achieve it.

I know from experience that if your mind is made up, you will commit to saving and then investing. If you are willing to take consistent, committed action, you will succeed. If you base your savings on the money principles I discuss later in the book and a budgeting model that suits you, you should get results. You should be able to save £10,000 or more over the next few years, and I look forward to your testimonial. The only thing you have to decide is how long it will take you based on your finances and level of commitment. I still went on holiday but within my budget. I still ate out at restaurants but within moderation. I spent money within my means, and when I did spend money, I knew I had budgeted for it. I would sacrifice eating out at work daily for eating out less often so that I could save more money. **Eating out every day at work can easily add up to £35 a week, and that can add up to a whopping £140 a month or £1,680 a year!** This includes things like sandwiches, crisps, pastries, cigarettes, soft drinks, coffee, hot chocolate, etc. A visit to a restaurant once or twice a month that costs £20 a time is a lot cheaper. You will have to bring food to work but just think of the health and financial benefits of home cooking. **To succeed, you will need to be willing to make a short-term sacrifice for a long-term gain.** I would prefer to save this money now and get it to work harder in my savings and investments so I can have a more comfortable life later on.

"Too many people spend money they haven't earned, to buy things they don't want, to impress people they don't like."

Will Smith

Habits

It is possible for you to save money on a low income. **The mindset you adopt will help you immensely. Your habits will cause you to succeed or fail.**

I have begun this chapter with a powerful quote from the American musician Will Smith. His statement is very true. People tend to buy things to impress others despite not caring about these people deep down. Alongside this, we tend to hold onto things we no longer require. If you look through your wardrobe or your trainer or shoe collection, how many of these items do you actually wear? Is there a lot of excess? I find that in western countries, in particular, we live lives of excess, and it costs us dearly both financially and at times emotionally, for example, through the impact of debt in our lives.

It is important to discuss habits in detail because your habits shape your life far more than you probably realise. Habits are very strong. In fact, our brains cling to them to the exclusion of all else – including common sense. Did you know that more than 40% of the actions you perform each day aren't actual decisions but habits? (www.sciencedaily.com). As such, we need to be mindful of our financial habits and create new, more helpful habits, such as saving regularly.

Not only are habits important. They grow stronger and stronger over time and become more and more automatic. So make sure you have the right ones! Habits are so powerful because they create neurological cravings. A certain behaviour is rewarded by the release of 'pleasure' chemicals in the brain. If a bad habit is created, you need to change it. You need to interrupt it and create a new one.

Saving as a habit

I encourage healthy habits, such as saving money on a weekly basis. We currently have three savings challenges that empower people of all income levels to save. You can begin saving with as little as £1 a week or more, depending on your income and circumstances. The goal is to make saving money habitual.

Below are some common bad habits that affect people's relationship with money.

Avoid these 10 habits at all costs:

1. Not saving money on a regular basis
2. Buying items you don't need
3. Making excuses for your financial situation
4. Not discussing money with others
5. Not building a big enough Freedom Fund aka Emergency Fund
6. Not investing money
7. Not budgeting
8. Living above your means

9. Not tackling debt. Debt is expensive and needs to go!

10. Wanting to keep up with the Joneses

Wealth Building Exercise: Write down three negative habits you want to change and replace them with a good new habit you want to develop. For example, you may not be saving money. Perhaps your new habit could be to begin saving money on a weekly or monthly basis.

A 2009 study by Phillippa Lally, a health psychology researcher at UCL, entitled *'How long does it take to form a habit',* found that **on average, it takes 66 days for a habit to become ingrained.** So the key is to be patient with yourself and not to expect results overnight. Be committed to slow and steady results, and if you make a mistake, just keep on going. The good habit will eventually manifest in your daily routine. Remember, it may take 66 days of continuous activity to convert a bad habit into a good habit.

Your WHY

Knowing **WHY** I want to achieve financial freedom has been crucial to my success in saving money. Let's discuss your why. **What is your WHY?**

The importance of your WHY!

I had a clear why and that is why I have been successful in saving money. I didn't want to experience debt. I didn't want to be poor and live pay-check to pay-check. I desired to be financially secure and independent. I have a strong financial vision and have set several big financial goals for my life that I am still in the process of achieving. I want to live in the suburbs in a spacious home and send my son to a private school should I choose to. I want to be able to travel the world whenever I choose, and to be able to give money to good causes. I want to pass down wealth to my family. I want to keep investing my money and to see my investments grow over the years before retiring in comfort, knowing that I am financially secure. This has motivated me and has caused me to handle my money well. Today I have a healthy, growing investment portfolio. Family, friends, and the wealth builders on the Rapid Wealth Building Platform are saving money daily, clearing debt, building their net worth, and are going on to invest confidently. You are welcome to join us. Imagine 100,000 like-minded individuals achieving this goal together. You can sign up at www.saverstoinvestors.com for a free 30-day trial.

What is your **WHY**? Why do you want to be financially secure? Why do you want financial stability? What will this mean for you and your family? **Your WHY needs to be heartfelt and needs to come from deep within**

you so that if temptation arises for you to spend unwisely, you can discipline yourself and say NO.

With this in mind, ask yourself WHY you want financial security or financial freedom. What is your big WHY? Take some time to think and reflect, then write down your answer.

....

....

....

....

....

....

The importance of goal-setting

Goal-setting is a key tool people use to achieve results. A lot of people have achieved things in life on the back of setting a clear, attainable goal. Goals can be professional, personal, financial, emotional. We will focus on financial goals. There is no better feeling than having accomplished a goal that you have set for yourself. This is how I was able to save a set amount of money each year and save £10,000 over several years. I continue to set financial goals, and I will do this for the rest of my life.

To achieve a goal, you need a plan. When an aeroplane leaves an airport, it has a destination in mind. It follows a plan. An aeroplane heading for Australia does not follow a route that will take it to Italy as its final destination. **If you do not follow a plan, you can end up anywhere! In debt, stranded, living pay-check to pay-check, having no savings, etc.!** What plan do you have in place for your finances? **What route are you following for your finances?** If you do not have goals or a plan in place, then let's begin to work on some. **The goal is to non-judgementally build wealth. To do so, we need a few goals to guide us along the way.**

Wealth Building Exercise: Your easy peasy financial task is to identify, write down, and share your goals. Set three goals for your finances. Before you set your goals, read the goal-setting tips below.

How to nail this task:

- List no more than three of your personal financial goals
- Be detailed with your goals
- Write down your goals and post them where you can see them daily. Create a vision board of your financial goals
- Share your goals with others (hold yourself accountable by sharing your goals)
- Get an accountability partner

An example to help you. You need to write down the goal and state:

1. **WHAT** do you want to achieve?
2. **WHEN** will you achieve it by?
3. **HOW** will you achieve it?

Example of a financial goal: I will save 10% of my salary each month

(What) I will save 10% of my wages every month.

(When) I will save 10% of my salary when I get paid on Tuesday 9 November 2021.

(How) I will save 10% of my money by **making an automatic payment** from the account that my salary gets paid into and pay this into my savings account.

Tip: *Find an accountability partner who will hold you accountable to your goals. Make sure you feel comfortable sharing your goals with them.*

Financial vision

What is your financial vision for your life?

Having a financial vision for yourself is very important. **This will give you secure foundations and allow you to**

aim for something specific. Create a vision board of your finances based on your financial goals. I have a vision board of my goals on my wall. My vision board constantly reminds me of my financial vision and motivates me to achieve what is on my vision board. The goals on my vision board are becoming a reality. You get what you focus on.

What is the financial vision you have for your finances?

....

....

....

....

....

....

How will you achieve it? What do you need to do?

....

....

....

....

....

....

NOTES PAGE

CHAPTER 2

MONEY PRINCIPLES

How can you save thousands of pounds a year?

I will share with you a budgeting model that **I still use today. It gives solid foundations to my savings. This solid foundation empowered me to save thousands of pounds per year on a low income, as a single parent.** If I can do it, so can you! Please tweak this model according to what suits you. Below is the budgeting model.

The budgeting model I used to save thousands of pounds a year

Generally, I set aside 10% or more of my income for saving and investing. I have fun or pay for things relating to personal development with 10%. I give 10% away to my church or to charity, and then I live off the remaining 70%.

I pay off all my household bills such as rent, council tax, internet, electricity, gas, gym, water bill, tuition fees, childcare fees, etc. with the 70% that is left over. If I choose to save or invest more than 10% each month it comes out of this 70%.

Caution: Please tweak these figures if necessary. You may need to prioritise debt, so you may need to reduce the money you have set aside for savings and investments, your fun fund, or good causes, if necessary, to pay any debt. Remember, clearing debt is the priority, as debt is expensive, but you should still keep a small portion of your money for savings while you are paying down debt. This is because you never know if an unexpected event may occur that requires money at short notice. The last thing you want is to take on more debt on top of the existing debt because you unexpectedly need more money. **This is why it's crucial to save money alongside paying down your debt.**

The key to your money success is repaying your debt as soon as possible and keeping it out of your life. The interest rate on your debt repayments is so high that it is <u>killing and crippling your potential for wealth</u>

based on the amount of interest you pay on it. (Typically, you pay 20.7% interest on most debt such as credit cards). You also have to spend a lot of your time physically working to pay off this overpriced, expensive debt! Would any bank give you a savings rate that high? **The goal is to get your money working hard for you through saving and investing, rather than your money working hard against you through debt!**

Key money principles

These are the three money principles that I actually used to save thousands a year for myself and my son. I still use these money principles alongside the budgeting model above.

1. Live off less than you earn

2. Pay yourself first at least 10%

3. Build a Freedom Fund – or Emergency Fund – of at least £1,000 or three to six months' income ideally.

1. Live off less than you earn

Many people do not get ahead financially because they do not live off less than they earn. Very few people manage money well. There is a statistic that states that one in four adults in the UK has no savings. (*The Independent*). **That**

is 25% of adults with no savings! It means 25% of adults have no prospect of early retirement or financial freedom! This figure is very shocking.

People either spend all they earn and have no savings, or they spend all the money they earn and then a bit more money on top, which is why they have debt. This debt is often built up by using credit cards, store cards, car finance, loans, or payday loans, etc.

The way to live off less than you earn is through budgeting. Budgeting gives you a bird's eye view of your finances. It helps you to see how much money comes in and how much money goes out. You can get a free budgeting sheet from my website www.saverstoinvestors.com. Make sure you fill out the budgeting sheet so you can see the current condition of your finances. I find it easy to live off less than I earn because I live from a budget and spend in cash as much as I can in order to control my expenditure. I do use my debit card for spending at times, but I try to spend in cash as much as possible. I avoid spending money from my debit card as it is easy to lose track of my spending if I can't see money physically leaving my purse or wallet. This allows me to budget more easily. I have a set amount each month to spend on food, clothing, eating out, etc. **Once the money is finished, it is finished. I leave no option for the use of credit cards or loans, etc, because I budget within my means. I also have my Freedom Fund to act as a**

financial buffer should I ever need money at short notice.

Wealth Building Exercise: Go through six to twelve months of your bank statements and audit your spending. What are you spending your money on? What common patterns are you spotting?

A lady called Fiona who did this exercise told me that she removed unnecessary subscriptions and eliminated £367 worth of unnecessary spending per month! She said she did this in one sweep. She felt relieved at all the extra money she had available to redirect towards saving. She was very grateful for the exercise. I heard another lady mention that she eliminated £300 worth of wastage per month using this method.

Generally, I monitor what I am buying and go through my bank statements monthly. I call the day I go through my finances a **Wealth Date**. My Wealth Date takes place once a month in the first week of the month. You may want to have a date with your finances once a week or once a month. This is a very good wealth-building habit to develop. We help people to have a Wealth Date with their finances by tracking our wealth builders' net worth once a month in an accountability session. Monitoring your finances is important as it allows you to see growth or a decline in your net worth. We will discuss the importance of net worth soon.

2. Pay yourself first at least 10%

The key point here is that you need to pay yourself first before you pay anyone else. So, before you pay any bills like your rent, mortgage, council tax bill, childcare bill, internet, Netflix, or mobile phone bill, etc, **you should guarantee you pay yourself first. The taxman pays himself first. He takes on average 20% from most workers before they even get paid by their employer!** You need to behave like the taxman and pay yourself 10% or more of your salary before paying expenses such as bills, gym, mobile phone bill, rent or mortgage, etc. This should ideally be no less than 10% of your salary. It can be as much as 20 to 25% depending on your income and overheads. **Make sure that this money is automatically taken from your account the day after you get paid. Treat this money like you are paying a bill.** Treat this money as a bill payment towards your financial freedom! **Pay the money into a separate bank account that you don't bank with.** This will help you to stop spending because it will be inconvenient for you to access the money if you have paid it into a bank you don't use.

Filling out the budgeting sheet from my website will allow you to figure out how much you can pay yourself first each month. **Remember, the taxman says he is worth at least 20%. What are you worth?**

3. Building a Freedom Fund aka Emergency Fund

It is important to build a financial safety net to protect yourself from financial hardships such as unexpected emergencies and getting into debt. Most people call this fund an Emergency Fund. I have renamed this pot of money a Freedom Fund because I believe that if you plan for an emergency, you will get an emergency, but if you plan for freedom, you will get freedom.

Helping people to build a Freedom Fund is my number one passion. This is because it has protected me from debt and the stress and frustrations that go along with it. I will share with you a personal story to demonstrate the power of building a Freedom Fund.

When I was 25, I gave birth to my young son Ashton. I moved into a spacious one-bedroom Victorian terraced flat in Peckham, South London. I was a single mum, so only one income was coming in. The flat was in very good condition and did not require any decorating, fortunately! However, the only furnishing inside this fairly spacious flat was a small fridge-freezer. **It dawned on me that I would need about £2,500 to furnish the whole flat!** I had to buy big household items like a cooker, washing machine, sofa, and television. I also needed a bed, cot, wardrobe, and drawers. I even needed small thing likes crockery, cutlery, and glassware. **I**

needed everything aside from a fridge-freezer. I am proud to say that on that day back in November 2011, when I moved into my flat, **I had the dignity of furnishing it without asking for any outside help because I had planned for my freedom.** Despite not knowing when a situation would arise that would require me to spend such a large amount of money unexpectedly, I was prepared. **I wasn't caught off-guard, and so *I never had debt.* Please build your Freedom Fund asap.**

I never thought I would need to furnish a flat all in one go. Because I managed my money well, I did not need to use a credit card or take a small loan to buy items for the flat. I didn't need to ask family or friends for money or write letters to charities asking for assistance. I'm sure you can see the freedom in having a safety net of money in place (your Freedom Fund). I am pleased to say that I am always prepared for unexpected financial situations. My Freedom Fund stops me from being vulnerable to debt and protects me from interrupting my savings or investments. This allows my money to keep working hard for me, so I do not have to work so hard for money.

There have been several times when I have needed to go into my Freedom Fund. I trust you can now see why I call it the Freedom Fund. It keeps you financially free and secure. When you spend this money, you will need to build it back up again. My Freedom Fund is worth £3,000, but yours can be as low as £1,000 or as high as three to six months' salary. **You should have full confidence that the amount you have saved is sufficient to cover you in any financial scenario.** This could include job loss, the unexpected need to travel at short notice, a car repair, boiler breakdown, or to cover household goods breaking down unexpectedly, such as the fridge-freezer, cooker, laptop, washing machine, etc.

I needed to use my Freedom Fund again when I moved from the one-bedroom flat in Peckham to a two-bedroom flat in Camberwell. This flat required lots of decorating and new laminate flooring and paintwork throughout. I also had to cover removal fees and pay to fully furnish my son's bedroom. I needed approximately £2,500. I had this money in place because of my replenished Freedom Fund, so I could get on right away with the decorating and furnishing! **I always make sure I replenish the Freedom Fund once I use it, and use it only when I absolutely need to**. Your Freedom Fund is an investment in yourself**. It gives you peace of mind.** Build this up to a minimum of £1,000 as quickly as possible, because it will protect you from debt and financial hardship. Once you have £1,000, aim to save 3 to 6 months' salary for ultimate peace of mind. **Speed is really of the essence as you never know when you will need money unexpectedly.**

Now that you know the key money principles to saving, and have a budgeting model in place, it is time to begin saving. The three money principles discussed earlier, and the budgeting model (that can be tweaked to suit your personal circumstances) will help you get results. And remember to stay consistent in saving, even when you are tempted to get distracted. You need to save money every month. Even if you have to reduce the amount a little now and again, depending on your circumstances. Saving a pound or a few pounds a week is better than saving nothing. This is why we have regular savings challenges on the Rapid Wealth Building Forum starting from £1 a week.

Indulging in new shoes, a bag, or a dream holiday will be tempting, but you can withstand the temptation in the long-term if you have a big WHY and a money goal. You need a constant reminder of WHY you are saving and you need a money goal you are working towards. It helps to back this up with a vision board that can remind you of the financial adventure you are now undertaking and the results you hope to achieve. Remember, if you need help on this financial journey, we can support you consistently and daily with solid financial literacy and accountability on the Rapid Wealth Building Platform.

NOTES PAGE

CHAPTER 3

SAVING MONEY

This book demonstrates how I saved over £10,000 on a low income. I saved over £10,000 for my son and myself over a period of several years. **Slow and steady can win the race!** You can take longer, or you may want to achieve this goal more quickly. The key to success is to **set a realistic money goal and put a solid plan in place to achieve it.** It took me eight years to save £10,000 for my young son, with the help of interest being added to his savings. I saved for him monthly in his Junior Cash ISA. I used a cash ISA because the money is tax-free, up to £4,368 per year. On average, my son was receiving 3% interest. I have had to be realistic in my own savings goal alongside the savings goal for my son. The key lesson is to be realistic with your finances. Pay yourself first at least 10% of your monthly income. **The goal ultimately is to earn more money so you can save more money and eventually begin investing more money.**

I wanted my son to have a head-start in life that I wasn't given. I began depositing small amounts into his cash ISA every month. I have done this since he was a few weeks old. I didn't notice this money was leaving my account because it was automated. It was a modest amount that slowly built up over time, tax-free, with the help of compound interest. When I hit the £10,000 mark for his savings, it felt like a victorious moment. My original goal was to save my son £10,000 before he reached the age of ten. I achieved this goal more than a year earlier. This was because of the effect of compound interest working on his finances over time. This was a slow and drawn-out journey but, 9 years later, I am pleased to say that I have given him a head-start in life. Not many people have achieved this goal, but it is very achievable. All children deserve a financial head-start.

Despite my passion for saving, my son's money has just been invested. The investment returns on average will be a lot higher than his savings account. I became my own investment guinea pig back in February 2019 when I began investing in funds based on my own research, and then under the guidance of a qualified financial adviser just for extra confidence. I can now invest quite confidently but still get advice for extra reassurance. Additional professional advice and support is a nice safety net. **I am frugal with money, but it stops at a certain point. I don't compromise on spending money on professional financial advice, and neither should you, as you should gain the money back in the performance of your investments over time.**

Being frugal

Being frugal is crucial to your financial stability. You need to live within your means. Being frugal doesn't have to be a permanent feature of your life. I do not plan to live frugally for the rest of my life. I regularly invest in my learning and development in order to upskill myself so that I can earn more money, so that I can save more, invest more, and buy more income-producing assets.

If you have a long-term plan for your finances, your savings, coupled with investing, should begin to create enough income for you to live better later on. This is summed up by the statement below:

"Earn more, save more, and buy income-producing assets."

Annette Galloway

I live frugally now so I have more money to save and invest in order to live better later on. I was willing to cut back on my expenditure on clothing and food, etc., to generate more money to save. I buy quality fresh food and non-branded food items so I can keep more money in my pocket. I buy good quality clothing that doesn't break the bank, so I shop in stores like H&M, Zara, Next, and New Look. I am also willing to shop for decent quality clothing in charity shops. I am quite stylish, but if I see a high-quality work shirt or blazer in a charity shop that I would be happy to pay full price for, it makes sense to purchase these items for a fraction of the price. The charity shops in Camberwell, South London, offer really nice, stylish clothing. Check them out!

Being frugal is important, but don't expect this to last forever. Once your money is working hard, you can increase your lifestyle within reason. Continue to budget your earnings using the budgeting model as a reference point. Change the model according to your needs and make sure your investments are receiving returns that allow you to achieve your financial goals. For example, you may have a goal for the amount of money you want to retire on. Will your current level of pension contributions make this retirement goal possible?

Being frugal – Top tips

1. **Be grateful and content** with what you have
2. Take lunch to work
3. **Know your budget**
4. **Use cash.** Leave your cards at home
5. **Buy non-branded goods** and shop in budget stores like Aldi and Lidl- I save a lot of money shopping in these stores, yet get good quality food and drinks

6. **Pay bills annually** to save money (car insurance, bus pass, travel card)

7. **Ask for a discount when your bills are up for renewal,** for example, mobile phone and internet contracts

8. **Shop around annually for competitive deals on regular household bills** such as gas and electricity

9. **Monitor your expenses monthly.** How much do you spend on sandwiches, coffee, cigarettes, alcohol, tea, sweet treats, etc.? Use a spending diary

10. **Are you still paying for items you don't use?** For example, gym membership, magazine subscriptions, etc. Get rid of these payments

11. **Have a Wealth Date with your finances** at least once a month

How many years does it take to save £10,000? The key point you need to be aware of is that before you save £10,000, you need to be debt-free. If you have debt, it is far wiser to repay it rapidly and begin saving £1,000 as quickly as possible. Once you have cleared debt and have £1,000 in place, then you can begin saving £10,000.

The length of time it takes you to save £10,000 depends on how much disposable income you have to save and also on how quickly you want to achieve this goal. Below I have listed how much you need to put away per month to save £10,000, from one year to ten years. I haven't factored in interest, but even a small amount of interest would help speed up your money's growth journey, due to the effect of compound interest. Remember, compound interest is good for your savings as it means you are earning interest on interest. **So make sure you save your money into an account that pays you the highest possible interest rate.** See the section on savings account rates discussed later in this chapter to learn what types of accounts pay the highest rates of interest.

Wealth Building Exercise: Choose the length of time you would like to save £10,000 over. You may want to do it in one year, or three years, or seven years, or ten years. Choose an option that suits you. – **Remember: Slow and steady can win the race.**

Choose what amount of money and timeframe suits your current financial situation when saving £10,000.

Duration	**Amount you need to save per month**
£10,000 in **1 year**	**£833.33 a month**
£10,000 in **2 years**	**£416.66 a month**

£10,000 in **3 years**	**£277.77 a month**
£10,000 in **4 years**	**£208.33 a month**
£10,000 in **5 years**	**£166.66 a month**
£10,000 in **6 years**	**£138.88 a month**
£10,000 in **7 years**	**£119.04 a month**
£10,000 in **8 years**	**£104.16 a month**
£10,000 in **9 years**	**£92.59 a month**
£10,000 in **10 years**	**£83.33 a month**

As you can see, you need to save money consistently every month. If you miss a month, that's ok. Just continue the following month and don't get too hung up about it. I missed payments occasionally if I needed to budget for something else, but this was rare. The best way to achieve results is to **automate the payment into a bank account that you don't use so that you can't see the money daily**. This reduces the temptation to spend it. Using a separate bank account will make it more difficult for you to access the money. This will also help you overcome the urge to spend the money as it won't be so accessible. **If you do get tempted to spend the money, remind yourself of your WHY and have a look at your financial goals and the financial vision you have made**

for your life, and re-commit to it. A Notice Savings account may be the best account if you struggle with temptation as you need to give the bank notice before you can take the money.

Once you have committed to the idea of saving, you need to begin saving. Many people know they need to save but they do not act, or they take action for a limited time and then default back to their old lifestyle of not saving and living pay-check to pay-check. This is the reason you need to find a strong and powerful WHY that will motivate you to want to save. My WHY was that I didn't want to be in debt like my mum and experience financial hardship. I wanted to make and achieve my money goals, such as living in the suburbs and having enough money to send my son to private school. I am still working on these goals, and that is the beauty of this journey. It is a long-term commitment. That is why we set goals and then begin to take action to achieve them, such as saving money on a regular basis. Below is a list of the different types of savings accounts that you can research to choose one that suits your personal needs.

Savings Accounts

There are several types of savings accounts that you can use to save in. Below is a list of the different types on offer and their typical annual interest rates:

1. **Regular Savings Accounts** – Typically pay up to 3%

2. **Childrens' Savings Accounts** – Typically pay up to 3%

3. **Easy Access Savings Accounts** – Typically pay up to 0.90%

4. **Notice Accounts** – Typically pay up to 1.00%

5. **Monthly Interest Accounts** – Typically pay up to 1.50%

6. **Fixed Rate Bonds** – Typically pay up to 1.65%

(Rates are average and are correct as of December 2020) The current rates can be found at www.moneyfacts.co.uk

Some of these accounts allow you to withdraw your savings right away with no penalty. Some will charge a penalty if you access the money too early. **Please read the terms and conditions of the account you are interested in carefully before opening the account and depositing your savings.**

Wealth Building Exercise: Visit the following website: **moneyfacts.co.uk/savings-account,** go through the savings accounts and choose an account that suits your personal needs. Pick an account that allows you to save cash at the highest possible interest rate.

I hope you have enjoyed learning about money management, and I hope you begin to apply all that you learn. You may feel empowered to do this alone. Fantastic. If you feel like you need some help and encouragement and want to join a community of like-minded wealth builders encouraging you to manage money better, then please join us for a free trial by signing up to the Rapid wealth Building Forum on the website at: www.saverstoinvestors.com

Savings Challenges

Save £1,000 as quickly as possible

For those of you who have big goals and want to save £10,000, that is fantastic. For those of you who want to save less, that is just as significant. **One of the main goals of the Rapid Wealth Building Platform is to get you to save £1,000 as quickly as possible, and to clear all consumer debt.** We encourage saving as a weekly habit, and we have **three savings challenges that run on average over 26 weeks.** When the 26 weeks are up, we roll the challenge over for another 26 weeks. We believe small amounts of money are just as valuable and significant as saving larger amounts of money daily. Hence you can begin saving a small amount of money or a larger amount of money.

We also encourage our wealth builders to monitor their net worth on a monthly basis so they can track it and begin building wealth. This encourages people to have healthy money habits, such as saving and budgeting. Once a wealth builder's financial literacy increases, we encourage them to invest, and provide the resources for them to do so safely and confidently.

KEY RESOURCES FOR SAVING AND BUDGETING

Savings Apps

Savings apps can help you automate your saving. This can make budgeting less stressful than using the traditional pen and paper method. If you want to use an app, the following can be helpful:

Chip

You can use this app to save spare change.

- Save and track your money automatically
- Create, track and allocate money to your goals
- Connects to your bank account in seconds

Monzo:

Monzo is a bank that is big on encouraging you to save. With this bank you can:

- Set savings goals
- Create savings pots that earn interest

Plum

Helps you save a larger amount of money, so it is ideal if you have a big savings goal.

- Plum analyses your transactions daily to learn about your income and spending.
- Plum automatically sets money aside. Every few days, Plum does the maths and transfers the perfect amount from your bank account. Little by little, it adds up.
- Be better off. Plum helps you set aside more, invest money, and stops you from being overcharged on bills.
- Lower your bills. £179/year – Average savings per customer on regular bills.

Budgeting Apps

Money Dashboard

Money Dashboard is an award-winning app that is **great for helping you budget for future goals.** It allows you to see all your accounts in one place. It categorises your spending, so you know where your money is going. The app also helps you to develop a savings plan.

- Award-winning app
- Has a budget planner that can set a budget
- Helps you to see where your money goes

Yolt

Yolt is an app that links all your bank accounts and credit card accounts, etc. **Yolt is great for allowing you to see all of your spending patterns and behaviour across several accounts.** Yolt helps you to:

- Spot and address bad money habits, like over-spending
- Shows all your transactions on all your accounts in one place

- Helps you to budget by tracking your spending
- Allows you to monitor bills and subscriptions

NOTES PAGE

CHAPTER 4

OVERCOMING DEBT

You need to kill your consumer debt

Not all debt is bad. Some businesses take on debt to invest in their operations and aim to pay back this debt using company profits they have made from taking on this debt. They plan to make profit from debt. This is a wise choice. The debt we are talking about killing today is consumer debt. **You literally pay a company to be in debt to them!** Consumer debt is debt like payday loans, credit cards, car finance, store cards, and bank loans. The interest rates are fairly high, especially on credit cards and payday loans. **Debt is the enemy of progress and is lethal.** This is why I state that you need to kill this debt, or it will kill your financial progress. You have to regard it as an enemy of your progress, pay it down and keep debt out of your life at all costs, because the average interest rate on consumer debt is a lot higher than the average interest you will be paid on your savings and investments.

The Danger of Debt

https://www.mbna.co.uk/support/extra-help-with-your-finances/persistent-debt.html

The picture relating to debt is courtesy of **www.mbna.co.uk**. They also have a debt calculator, which will help you to calculate the impact of debt. You will find that the longer you pay minimum payments on your debt, the longer and more expensive it will be to pay back the debt. The graphic shows a credit card that has an interest rate of 24%. The person borrows £3,000. If they make minimum payments of £84 a month on the £3,000 they borrow, they will pay back a whopping £7,367 over fourteen years and eleven months! They will pay back £4,367 in interest! That is more than double the money borrowed! This does not make sense financially, and is why you need to live within your means.

If you increase the payment beyond the minimum amount and pay back £124 a month, the debt will cost a lot less at £3,981, and you can pay it off in two years and nine months. You will end up paying back £981 in interest. So what option would you take? Would you pay back more than double the amount you borrowed by only making minimum payments? Or would you pay back as much as you can and rapidly speed up the length of time you repay this debt? The choice is yours.

The picture above clearly demonstrates that by increasing your payment by a few pounds, there is a real knock-on effect in terms of the amount of time it takes to pay back the debt. The moral of the story is to **pay more than the minimum repayment so that you clear off debt quickly because debt is expensive! DON'T BE A DEBT SLAVE.** Learn how to master money and get it to be your slave instead. One way to achieve this is through investing and living within your means.

When you have debt in your life, you're a prisoner to that debt until you repay it. The only one truly benefiting is not you or your family, but the owner of the debt. You are practically a slave to Mastercard, or Visa, or to the company you are in debt to, as you are constantly making payments and not benefiting from these payments. **If you want to build wealth or pass on wealth, get rid of debt as soon as possible.** (See a list of organisations at the end of this book that can help you clear debt.)

Overcoming debt

Plan how you will overcome your debt and commit to getting out of debt and seek help if necessary. You will need to list all your debts with the interest rate you are paying. This will help you to see the true extent of your debt and to come to terms with it. You can then begin tackling your debts one by one.

Two methods to pay down debt:

1. The Debt Avalanche Method: Pay off the debt with the highest interest rate first and work your way down to the next highest interest rate debt. Eventually, you will reach the debt with the lowest interest, and you will clear that off, and then you will be debt-free!

For example, you will need to list all of your debts:

- Credit card 1 (20.93% APR) £600
- Credit card 2 (21.9% APR) £700
- Store card (30% APR) £350
- Payday loan (1003.90% APR) £650

You would then reorder them from highest interest rate to lowest interest rate.

1. Payday loan (**1003.90% APR**) for the amount of £650

2. Store card (**30% APR**) £350

3. Credit card 2 (**21.9% APR**) £700

4. Credit card 1 (**20.93% APR**) £600

In this case, you would pay off the payday loan first because it has the highest rate of interest at 1003.90% APR. You would then pay off the store card next because the interest rate is 30% APR. You would then pay off credit card 2 with the APR of 21.95%. You would clear the debt on credit card 1 last because it has the lowest interest rate at 20.93%.

2. The Debt Snowball Method: The Debt Avalanche Method is very similar to the Debt Snowball. **The difference is that you order your debts not by their interest rate but by the actual amount of debt you owe.** You pay off the lowest debt first and then work your way up to the next highest debt and so forth. You eventually tackle the biggest debt last.

The list of debts built up:

- Credit card 1 (20.93% APR) £600

- Credit card 2 (21.9% APR) £700

- Store card (30% APR) £350

- Payday loan 1003.90% APR for the amount of £650

So, taking our list our list of debts that have been built up, you would pay them off beginning with the lowest debt first and work your way up to the highest debt last:

1. Store card (30% APR) **£350**

2. Credit card 1 (20.93% APR) **£600**

3. Payday loan 1003.90% APR for the amount of **£650**

4. Credit card 2 (21.9% APR) **£700**

When applying the Snowball Method, you would begin by first paying off the store card at £350, then you would move on to credit card 1, at £600. You would then pay off the payday loan for the amount of £650. Credit card 2, which is the biggest debt at £700, would be paid off last.

Debt Stacking Concept. Here are the debt stacking steps:

Make minimum monthly payments to ALL your creditors. When one debt is paid in full, apply the amount you were previously paying to the next debt you have targeted to pay off. Apply this to the Avalanche Method or the Snowball Method.

Ultimately it makes sense to use **The Avalanche Method** and clear the highest interest rate debt first using the concept of Debt Stacking and work your way down to the next highest debt, as this is costing you the most money.

Emotionally it's statistically proven that you will succeed with the Snowball Method as you will enjoy the success of your small wins. It will give you lots of encouragement along the way. I have found that most people succeed with the Snowball Method as they become empowered by small wins. It motivates them to go on and tackle the next highest debt once they have successfully tackled the smallest debt on their list.

Tip: *Make sure that as you are tackling your debt, you make minimum payments on all other debts.* ***This makes sure that you do not get any further penalties on your existing debts.***

- Aim to be debt-free and to stay debt-free.
- Live from a budget.
- Remind yourself of WHY you want financial security.
- Buy things intentionally.
- Have strong financial goals and a financial vision to back it up.

- Refuse to be a debt slave.

You should not be a slave to money by constantly having to pay off debt. Have a no-nonsense attitude to debt.

Wealth Building Exercise: List all the debts you owe and note the interest rate you are currently paying. Add up the total amount of debt that you owe. You now have a clear figure to work with. **(Do this non-judgementally. You have decided to take positive action and tackle your debt, so give yourself a pat on the back.)**

All the debts I owe	The interest rate I am paying on the debt (%)

Wealth Building Exercise: Make a vow to yourself that you **will acknowledge your debts non-judgementally** and will commit to paying them off.

Pledge to Debt Freedom

I ……………………………………....... (insert name) promise that I will list and acknowledge all my debts, and I commit to paying them off by ………………………………2021/22.

I believe I can live debt-free and accept a life of debt freedom. I commit to seeking professional help if necessary and will commit all my effort to eliminating my debt.

I currently owe £…………………in debt, and **I commit to paying off this debt in full and remaining debt-free.**

Debt tips:

1. Stop creating more debt.
2. **Build an freedom fund/emergency fund to £1,000 as quickly as possible.** Stops you from going further into debt.

3. Increase your monthly debt payments. **Pay beyond the minimum payment, ESPECIALLY ON HIGH-INTEREST DEBT.**

4. **How much do you owe? Who do you owe?** Get help with a debt repayment plan. This should list all your creditors, how much you owe, the interest rate being charged. Prioritise the debt, for example, note if there is a timeframe on the debt. Also, note which is your highest interest rate debt.

5. **Start a side hustle.** Find a way to bring in more money to use towards tackling the debt.

Being debt-free. Track your spending

The next step to getting out of debt is to keep **track of how much you're spending each month and then figure out where you can reduce spending.** Online tools and budgeting software (check out apps as well) can help you track your spending. Apps like Yolt are quite good. Or, if you prefer a more hands-on method, simply use paper and pen, or set up a spreadsheet to track your spending for 30 days. You can also use my budgeting spreadsheet that is listed on my website to get an idea of what income is coming in and what income is going out: www.saverstoinvestors.com

Keeping a spending diary may seem like a pointless exercise. However, **by keeping track of every single penny** that leaves your purse or wallet, you will get a good understanding of what actually happens to your money after it leaves your bank account.

Keeping a spending diary for at least a month will help you to see if there are any patterns with your spending. It's these patterns that will start to help you address some of your unnecessary spending and help you understand what you can stop spending money on.

For example, if you find you buy a coffee from a café every Tuesday morning and it costs you £3 (remember that's £156 a year), you may find that buying a travel mug and taking your own drink will help you break a costly habit you may not have realised you had.

Wealth Building Exercise: Print out six months of your bank statements and look for patterns and trends in how you spend your money. Categorise the spending, for example, eating out, clothing, transport, bills, rent, mortgage, etc. Spending insights: What type of spender are you? Frugal, balanced, or excessive? Will you hit your money goals long-term and short-term if you continue spending like this?

Questions to ask yourself. Are you overspending and using an overdraft? Are you buying needs or wants? **An app like Yolt can help you get a perspective of your**

spending. Yolt is great because it allows you to see all of your spending patterns and behaviour across several accounts. Yolt helps you to spot and address bad money habits, like over-spending, and helps you to budget by tracking your spending.

The goal of this book is to get you saving £10,000. Before you save £10,000 on a low income, you will need to save £1,000 as quickly as possible and be debt-free because debt is expensive and needs to be paid back at high rates of interest. You will be a wealthier person all around if you pay down your debt quickly. You need to get rid of the wastage of your finances that debt causes. Debt is literally like pouring money down a plug hole!

NOTES PAGE

CHAPTER 5

IMPROVING YOUR CREDIT SCORE

Your credit score is a reflection of your relationship with money. **Your credit score determines how expensive credit will cost you.** It allows banks and institutions that borrow you money (credit) to make a decision about your credit-worthiness. They look at your credit score and decide whether or not they trust you to pay them the money back on time. If your credit score is high, you can obtain credit easily, and it is more affordable. If your credit score is low, you may struggle to obtain credit, and when you do obtain credit, the rates of interest may not be as competitive as those offered to people with higher credit scores. As such, you need to improve your credit score so that you can get better rates of credit.

Why is credit important?

At times in your life, you may need to use credit to make certain purchases such as a home, to fund a wedding, or a car purchase, etc. To get competitive rates of credit, you need to obtain a good credit score and maintain a good credit history.

With a good credit score, you are able to:

- Qualify for lower interest rates and higher credit limits
- Access better deals on credit cards, mortgages, and loans
- Improve your chances of being accepted by a landlord if you want to rent a property
- Get cheaper car insurance rates (when paying monthly for cover)
- Secure utility services without a deposit or 'letter of guarantee'

Ultimately, with a better credit score, lenders will see you as a lower risk, and you are therefore more likely to be accepted for credit.

It is important for you to have an idea of what your credit score actually is. This will allow you to improve it if necessary. If you need to improve your credit score, you will need to start taking action. I will share with you some tips that have helped clients to build their credit score higher.

What is your current credit score?

In order to improve your credit score, you need to find out what your current score is. You can access a **free copy** of your report on Experian.

Wealth Building Exercise: Find out what your credit score is and commit to improving it if necessary. Visit the Experian website to find out what your current credit score is. *www.experian.com*

My credit score is……………………

Bonus tip: Sign up to Experian Boost and boost your credit score very quickly.

Experian Boost allows consumers to add additional on-time payments to their credit report at Experian by linking their bank account. Experian Boost is a free service to anyone with an Experian account. It allows consumers to add additional data to their credit histories, such as bill payments for services like Netflix, their mobile phone bill, etc., with the goal of improving their FICO scores. FICO is currently the credit scoring model most widely used by lenders.

Ways to improve your credit score

There are many ways to improve your credit rating and creditworthiness, including the following:

- **Pay your bills on time**
- **Spend on your credit card little and often**
- **Register on the electoral roll**
- **Close any unused accounts**
- **Limit your credit applications**
- **Only borrow what you can afford to repay**
- **Keep your credit card balances low (the use of your credit facility should be below 30%)**
- **Clear excessive credit card debt**
- **Check your credit report often**

How long will it take to improve your credit score?

How long it takes to build a good credit score depends on a wide range of factors, but the most important thing to remember is that it won't happen immediately.

Improving your credit score is a long-term process, which is why most people are urged to start **building a credit history from an early age**. Once you start making changes by using the methods listed above, you should see your credit score climb over time.

For example, information about new credit cards or bank accounts can take up to three months to reach Experian.

It can take a few months to see any real improvement on your credit report, but make no mistake, every method of building a better credit score that I have mentioned is worth considering, as they are all proven to work eventually.

NOTES PAGE

CHAPTER 6

BUILDING YOUR NET WORTH

"Earn high, spend low, and buy income-producing assets."

Annette Galloway

This quote has been mentioned earlier. The key point here is that you need to earn as much as you can, keep your spending low, and then buy income-producing assets. You also need to remember that you are not what you earn each year, but what you actually manage to keep.

"It's not how much money you make, but how much money you keep, how hard it works for you, and how many generations you keep it for."

Robert Kiyosaki

So, what is your net worth?

Your net worth is a reflection of you totalling up all your assets and taking away all of your liabilities. The goal is to build up your net worth and to keep it growing. Net worth is a very important financial concept. **It tells you how much you are actually worth.** Your actual net worth is the amount of money you have left once you have paid out all your expenses.

If Michael earns £80,000 a year and spends £80,000 a year, Michael has a zero net worth. If Ashton earns £25,000 a year and saves £6,000, Ashton's net worth will be £6,000. Ashton will be worth more than Michael, who is on a £80,000 salary, because Michael has not managed to save any of his money. **Remember it is not what you earn that matters but how much you keep.** If a person has debt, they will have minus 0 net worth. This is why debt has to go. It keeps you out of the wealth race.

It is crucial to clear consumer debt very quickly and begin building your net worth. This is why we track people's net worth monthly on the Rapid Wealth Building Forum. You need to build your net worth. Most people working a day-job talk of how much income they earn. Wealthy people speak about their net worth. Their net worth is ever-growing, fluctuating, and expanding, which is why the net worth of high-income individuals tends to be an estimation. They have so many income-producing assets working on their behalf that it is difficult to pin down their net worth to a specific number at any given time.

Net worth is estimated by taking the value of everything you own, **such as possessions that put money in your pocket (assets)**, and subtracting everything you owe, **such as possessions which take money out your pocket (liabilities),** for example, credit card debt, student loans, payday loans, car finance, and credit card debt, etc.

The aim is to increase your net worth through saving and investing, and by keeping yourself out of debt. Your goal is to increase your income by buying income-producing assets and reducing your liabilities as much as possible.

Remember: **It is not how much you earn that matters, but HOW MUCH YOU KEEP! What are you keeping?**

Below is the equation for net worth:

(Assets – Liabilities = Net Worth)

What are the examples of assets that increase your net worth?

Your assets are anything you own, such as:

- Cash
- Collectibles like gold and silver
- Real estate or investment property
- Land
- Cars/vans/motorbikes (These tend to depreciate in value year on year)
- Stocks and shares, also known as equities/funds
- Bonds/Gilts
- Household goods, for example, laptop, fridge-freezer, washing machine, sofa, etc. (Bear in mind these items are also depreciating assets as they lose value very quickly. The market price will be a lot less than what you paid as they will be regarded as second-hand goods).

***Tip**: Not all assets are the same. Some assets depreciate in value over time, such as cars, motorbikes, household goods, etc. The goal is to buy assets that tend to generate* *income over time, such as gold, silver, land, property, bonds, gilts, stocks and shares, etc.*

Now let's discuss liabilities you may have that decrease your net worth:

- Bank loans
- Mortgages
- Car finance
- Credit card debt
- Store card debt
- Payday loans
- Student loans
- Income tax debt

The goal is to build up your asset column and reduce your liability column. Now that you know the definition of net worth and can tell the difference between an asset and a liability, you **need to calculate your actual net worth.**

Note: The goal is to earn high, spend low and buy income-producing assets.

Wealth Building Exercise: List all your assets and all your liabilities. How much are you actually worth?

Assets	Liabilities

Remember: Assets – Liabilities = Net Worth

My total assets: £..............

My total liabilities: £..............

My net worth is: £..............

If you need help building your net worth, we can assist you on the Rapid Wealth Building Platform, where we track net worth monthly. We have a free 30-day trial that will empower you to begin building your net worth. You can sign up at www.saverstoinvestors.com and learn how to build wealth by eliminating debt, saving money, tracking your net worth, investing, and more.

Once you have cleared all consumer debt and have saved at least £1,000, or three to six months' salary, you are ready to begin building your net worth through investing.

NOTES PAGE

CHAPTER 7

GET A SIDE HUSTLE OR INCREASE YOUR EMPLOYED INCOME

The quickest way to increase your income and to help you build your net worth is to get a pay rise in your employed work, or to create an income-producing side hustle. This extra money can be used toward paying debt or putting towards your savings and eventually, investments. If you work fulltime, you can spend the hours outside of your working hours working on your side hustle.

How do you find a side hustle?

You may want to work on building something that you are already good at or are very passionate about that you can earn money from. In order to find yourself a suitable side hustle, ask yourself some questions:

- What are you genuinely interested in?

- What problem can you solve that someone will pay you to do for them?
- How can you add value to someone? In what ways? List them.

Make sure you define a clear goal when beginning your side hustle. You don't want to spend too much time and money on it only to find that no one requires that service. Take baby steps, for example, sell to one customer first and get feedback, and then sell to more customers before you become heavily invested in the idea. You need to make sure there is a real need for what you are doing. When you are convinced that there is a need, build your side hustle further. Remember, Rome was not built in one day. It may take time to get a solid base of supportive customers around your side hustle, but once it is established there is no reason why it shouldn't grow and expand and become a regular income stream. This may take a few years to build up, so don't be alarmed by slow growth.

NOTES PAGE

CHAPTER 8

THE IMPORTANCE OF INVESTING

Saving money is important to your financial well-being, however the key to your financial freedom is investing. When I was 23, back in 2009, I took out my first investment with a popular high street bank in Peckham South London. I invested £500 a month. I expected to get returns that were more competitive than the savings rate at the time, which was about 3% on average.

I invested £500 a month, and I did this for twelve months. When I asked the financial adviser what I was investing in, I was shown a paper that listed what looked like hundreds of names across different sectors. It felt like I was looking at a language I had never read before and being told to make sense of it. I asked what it meant, and the financial adviser told me I had bought a slice of cake. I told him that it looked like a lot of cake! Beyond that, I wasn't advised about my risk profile or that I needed to stay invested for several years, typically three to five, to get a decent level of growth. This would have caused me to stay invested. I wasn't told of the expected rate of returns or the importance of diversification. No one I knew of in my family or community was an investor, and I had never been taught financial literacy. As you can imagine, I was frustrated, and I'm sure many of you can relate to this frustration!

I stayed invested for twelve months. When I received the paperwork for the investment, I wasn't impressed by the performance of the investment. The financial adviser wasn't able to communicate to me effectively why the investment hadn't surpassed the 3% mark I expected it to. I was not able to have a beneficial conversation with the adviser, as I had no knowledge or understanding about investments other than the desire to invest. Due to this bad initial experience, I delayed investing again for nearly ten years. I decided to teach myself the investment basics. I wanted to feel empowered when having a conversation with a financial adviser, and I also wanted to begin D.I.Y investing for myself. I have fallen in love with D.I.Y investing. It has taken me more than a decade to get to this stage, but it was worth the wait in terms of my progress and development. I wouldn't want you to wait for so long. This is why I am so passionate about teaching wealth builders the basics of investing, as I know people delay investing because they are confused by the subject, just like I was.

I have gained confidence in my own investments, and they are doing very well. Far higher than the average savings account. Decent returns can be achieved for most people, provided they have enough financial literacy or get good financial advice from a qualified, experienced financial adviser. If anyone needs financial advice, please feel free to contact Edem Amewowor, whom I work alongside. He is a qualified financial adviser, based in London, who is passionate about what he does. Alternatively, approach a credible investment firm.

I am now in a privileged place where I can confidently make the most out of the world of investing. My life's mission is to help other people to access this powerful arena. I have seen a lot more growth in my wealth-building journey in investing than I ever could have achieved by saving alone. I hope with good financial literacy and advice, you will see similar results.

Inflation

The problem with saving is that inflation causes your money to lose value over time. Inflation means that the pound in your pocket is getting weaker and weaker year on year. See the example below for an understanding of why inflation is so lethal.

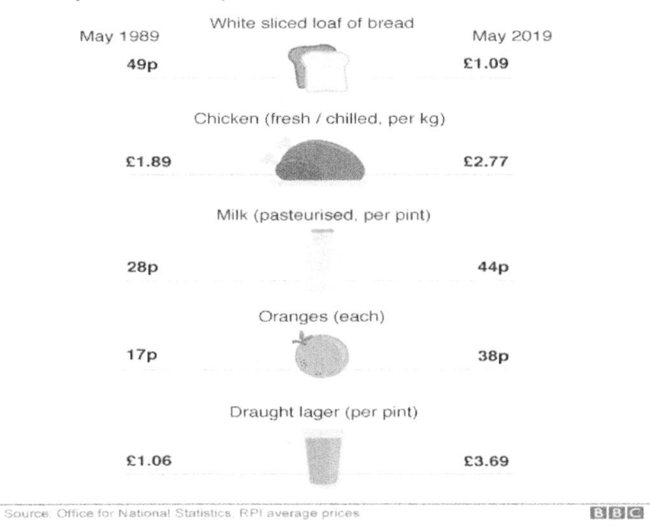

In the image above, you can see that a pound is still a pound, but that in May 1989 bread cost 49p, while 20 years later it doubled in price to £1.09p! If you are not investing your money, you will struggle to keep up with inflation, and you will find that life becomes more expensive every year. Another example is the cost of railway ticket prices going up annually. If your money is not working hard for you through saving and investing, then you will find it has to stretch further. This can be quite a strain. Investing is one way to combat the impact of inflation on your finances. We can help you invest safely by giving you a breakdown of what investing involves, and by helping you to find qualified financial advisers who can help you to invest.

Investing is what keeps the wealthy, wealthy, due to the potential for income and capital gains growth. If you're only saving, you're like a child riding a bike with stabilisers. To be truly independent on a bike, the child needs to learn how to ride without stabilisers. This is the equivalent of moving from being a saver to an investor and beginning to invest. You may be unsteady at first, but with practice you will master investing.

Compound Interest

Compound interest is one of the most powerful financial concepts you can get working in your finances. **The definition of compound interest is: Earning interest on interest. Einstein called it the 8th wonder of the world.**

There is a negative side to compound interest when it is applied to your debt, as discussed before. There is also a positive side to compound interest, which has the capacity to generate financial freedom in your life.

The image below demonstrates why I champion investing so much. I encourage people to begin saving and paying debt as quickly as possible so that they can begin to build their net worth through investing.

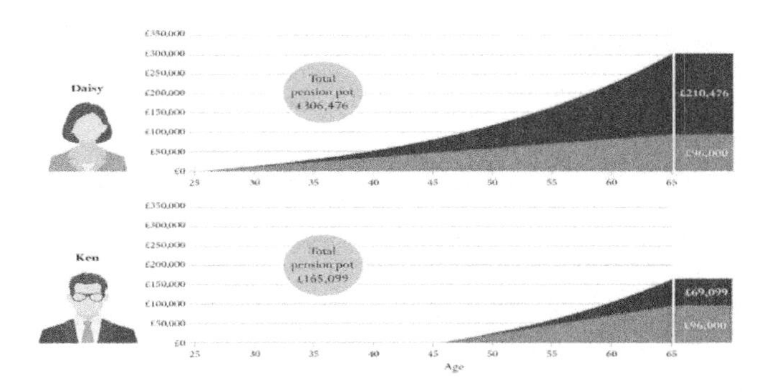

The chart illustrates how much difference compounding can make when someone starts saving earlier. Daisy starts saving £200 a month when she is 25; Ken saves £400 a month from the age of 45. In total, they both save £96,000 by the age of 65. However, assuming an illustrative growth rate of 5%, Daisy ends up with almost twice as much as Ken due to 20 extra years of compounding returns. The key lesson is that the quicker you repay debt, begin to save and then begin to invest, the quicker you get your money working hard for you.

What does it take to transition from being a person who just saves, to a person who invests?

Below is a summary of what you need to achieve in order to move from being a saver to being an investor.

You will need to:

- Clear all consumer debt, like credit cards, bank loans, etc. (I know you can do this!)

- Save at least £1,000, or three to six months' expenses before you invest
- Set a financial goal
- Have a financial vision for your life
- Know your WHY

When you are paying down debt and have your Freedom Fund of at least £1,000 or three to six months' salary, congratulations, you are ready to invest!

Please note: The goal of investing is to increase your capacity to create passive income. This is income that you earn while you sleep. You do not have to be actively present to earn it. Investing is an excellent way to generate this income.

Asset Classes

When you invest, there are seven asset classes you can invest in. Your goal is to create a diverse portfolio of these asset classes that take into account your risk profile. Seek professional advice from a qualified adviser if necessary.

The goal is to get as many of these asset classes working in your finances as quickly possible. We explore these asset classes in detail on the Rapid Wealth Building Platform.

The seven asset classes are:

1. Cash (Savings)
2. Equities/stocks and shares
3. Bonds/fixed-income assets
4. Cryptocurrency
5. Commodities such as gold, silver, coffee, oil, etc.
6. Collectibles such as antiques, cars, stamps
7. Investment property and real estate

Diversifying risk in your investments

As you can see, there are several asset classes you can invest in. When you begin to invest, you need to be aware of your risk profile and your tolerance to risk. You will also need to know how to diversify your investments so that you can reduce as much risk as possible. One way of doing this is by first investing in funds and not in individual stocks and shares. The reason for this is that funds are a lot more diversified, so the risk involved is less. You will also need to understand key investment terminology to become a confident investor. If you need more help learning where to invest, how to invest, or what to invest in, then please sign up for *Part 1: Mastering Financial Literacy and an Introduction to Investing*. See the website for further details: www.saverstoinvestors.com

I am sure by now you appreciate the need to set some money goals, repay expensive debt quickly, save money, build your net worth, and then begin investing. We are here to help if you need further support. Below is a quick summary of how I have become financially secure.

Summary – How I achieved my goal of saving £10,000

1. I PAID MYSELF FIRST! This is key
2. I saved monthly and automated my savings
3. I had a vision for my financial life
4. I was disciplined and stuck to a BUDGET
5. I mainly spent money in cash
6. I tracked my income. I knew what was coming in and what was going out
7. I followed a budgeting model
8. I knew my WHY (I know WHY I want what I want)

9. I didn't take on consumer debt like credit cards, store cards, and loans

10. I set financial goals

After reading this book, you should now be able to:

- Develop a positive mindset towards money
- Save money on a regular basis
- Build a Freedom Fund aka Emergency Fund of at least £1,000 or three to six months' salary
- Have financial goals
- Budget and live off less than you earn
- Repay debt rapidly
- Know your credit score
- Know your net worth and begin tracking it
- Be willing to invest your money and seek advice if necessary
- Be financially literate

Congratulations on reaching this far in the book. I hope you have learnt a lot. There are several things you can do to help yourself move further forward with your finances. Below are some suggestions for additional support.

Tips for further growth

- **Join a financial community.** This will empower and motivate you to get results. It should also help you to be accountable. I run the Rapid Wealth Building Platform if you are interested in joining. Further details are on our website, where you can join for a free 30-day trial.
- **Hire a coach, financial coach, mentor, lifestyle coach.** My coach asks me questions like who do you need to become to attract what you want? Feel free to reach out to me if you would like help with your finances.
- **Question what you buy**. Do you really need it or do you just want it? Only buy what you need, unless you have budgeted for what you want.

Read books like:

- *The Richest Man in Babylon* by George Clason
- *Think and Grow Rich* by Napoleon Hill
- *As a Man Thinketh* by James Allen

- *Rich Dad Poor Dad* by Robert Kiyosaki
- *Secrets of the Millionaire Mind* by Harv Eker
- *The Compound Effect* by Darren Hardy

Testimonials:

Thanks to you, Annette, I was motivated to get up at 5am and go through my finances. I have managed to make planned cuts (unused subscriptions, coffee shop habits, some luxuries) totalling a crazy £367 a month. **-Fiona**

I've started to allocate myself 10% of my income, which is a nice feeling. I have established my three financial goals. I have become more mindful of where and when I shop. I look for cheaper alternatives. I've cancelled a couple of direct debits, and reduced my Sky bill by £17. **-Sam**

The Rapid Wealth Building Forum is a great community of like-minded people who want to create wealth and manage their money more effectively. I have been budgeting and increasing my net worth through the learning received. I have created an emergency fund of £1,000, which was an early goal. Now working towards building an emergency fund which contains 3-6 months of my income. My knowledge in stocks and shares has grown, which has permitted me to invest in the stock market. A satisfied member. **-Amelia**

I thought my life was too busy to budget. I now enjoy budgeting because of the teaching I received. Because I now budget, I can step back and think before I buy. I now don't waste so much money. **-Fola**

Annette, you are helping me to save. I haven't done so in years. It's a small amount of savings, but it feels good to save. **-Tina**

I have been working on a budget, which has helped. I just kept on following your advice to build an emergency fund and pay off my debt. I do feel relieved. I need to work on building my savings now. **-Aurelle**

Since joining and learning about how to save effectively, I've set myself a personal target of saving £5,000 before the end of December 2020. Learning about the concept of paying myself when I get my wages has been revolutionary. Every week (as I get paid weekly), I pay myself a regular amount with the view of reaching my target by the end of December 2020. I have so far saved £4,300. We're now in November 2020, and I'm pretty certain that by December, I'll reach my target of having £5,000 in savings. Thank you for all you've taught me. I only joined your group less than nine months ago, but the progress I've made this far is tremendous. Thank you for your invaluable encouragement and knowledge impartation. - **Isabelle**

Some useful organisations that can help you clear debt:

Step Change Debt Charity

- www.stepchange.org

Step Change Debt Remedy provides you with the expert advice, budget support, and solutions to help you manage your debts.

Pay Plan

- www.payplan.com

Pay Plan's supportive, non-judgemental team of advisers help thousands of people beat their debts every year and treat all of their calls with the strictest confidence.

Debt Advice Foundation

- www.debtadvicefoundation.org

Debt Advice Foundation is a national debt advice and education charity offering free, confidential support and advice to anyone worried about debt.

Citizens Advice Web Chat

- www.citizensadvice.org.uk

Citizens Advice offers free, independent, confidential, and impartial debt advice through their webchat service.

Christians Against Poverty

www.cap.org

Christians Against Poverty are a Christian charity that is a national organisation specialising in debt counselling for people in financial difficulty, including those in need of bankruptcy or insolvency advice.

We hope you choose the right debt method and seek help and support if necessary.

I hope that this book has empowered you to save money so that you can go on and eventually invest money. **We trust you have enough material to help you to manage money well, but if you need further help, do not hesitate to get in touch.** Please find my details below.

And remember:

"Action is the foundational key to all success."

Pablo Picasso

Take action!

Best wishes,

Annette Galloway

Your Fellow Wealth Builder

Stay in touch:

Website: www.saverstoinvestors.com

Instagram: savertoinvestor

Email: info@saverstoinvestors.com

Tel: +44(0)7903 687 861

Printed in Great Britain
by Amazon